Bristol Radical Pamphl

A Brief History Of Corporations

Where Did They Come From?

Daniel Bennett

ISBN 978-1-911522-04-1

Bristol Radical History Group. 3rd Edition 2017.
1st Edition 2009.
www.brh.org.uk ~ brh@brh.org.uk

Introduction

How did the Commercial Corporation begin? How did Corporations[1] become able to act so freely? What rights do the public have in a democracy to challenge or control the actions of Corporations?

The first Commercial Corporation was created by direct unlawful action by the members of the company. From that date onwards our democratic right to control what Corporations do has been eroded and diminished until no control remained at all. Corporations and Governments have defined this erosion of control as being the liberation of Corporations from the shackles of the past. Corporations have achieved this "liberation" by breaking the law on mass until the Courts and the Government gave up trying to control them.

The State (through the Government and the Courts) has:

1. Abandoned rules which forbade the creation and continuance of Corporations that acted in a manner that caused the public harm (introduced in 1720 – repealed 1825);

2. Abandoned state control over the types of business operation that could become Corporations (finally abandoned in 1844);

3. Restricted then abolished the right of anyone who isn't the "Corporation"[2] to challenge the right of the Corporation to take various courses of action (abolished by the Companies Act 1989); and Transferred from the Government to the Courts and then to the Directors of the Corporation itself the final say over what any Corporation has the power to do.

4. A Corporation is special because by becoming a Corporation (a process called "incorporation"), a thing is given a distinct legal identity separate from the people who run it. This shields those who actually run the business from responsibility for their actions.

The Corporation

When using the term "Corporation" we are concerned with "business associations" that become Corporations. A "business association" is any association of people with the common objective of earning a profit. Contributing either capital (money) and/or labour each "partner" or "shareholder" receives a share of the profits commensurate to their contribution and bargaining power.

---

1 From now on, when the term Corporation with a capital C is used, I mean only Commercial Corporations.
2 Remember, a Corporation is a person before the eyes of the law.

When we talk about companies we are talking about Commercial Corporations. The term "company" originates from the term "joint stock company", and means the same thing as the term Commercial Corporation. A non-corporate "business association" is not a company at all but a partnership or a cooperative.

A Corporation is special because by becoming a Corporation (a process called "incorporation"), a business association is given a distinct legal identity separate from the people who run the business. Rather than people carrying out business in their own name, a Corporation is considered to be a person in its own right. The Courts, when dealing with a Corporation, accept the "fiction" that the Corporation has a birth, a death and more importantly, entitlement to human and civil rights. A Corporation, which exists solely on paper, can assert that, as a "person" it has the right to do something and that that right can prevail over another real person's right to object.

Rather than people carrying out business in their own name, a Commercial Corporation is considered to be a person in its own right. The Courts, when dealing with a Corporation, accept the fiction that the Corporation has a birth, a death (although a corporation can live forever) and more importantly, entitlement to human and civil rights. A Corporation, which exists solely on paper, can assert that it has the right to do something (e.g. pollute) and that that right can prevail over a real person's right to object.

A Commercial Corporation can create for itself a multiple personality with separate Corporations (all owned by the same parent Corporation) existing simultaneously. All risky and dangerous operations carried out by Corporations are carried out by subsidiaries. The parent Corporation, being only a shareholder in the subsidiaries (and therefore a separate legal person) cannot in any way be held responsible for the actions of the subsidiary[3]. These subsidiaries (and/or their immediate if not ultimate parent Corporations) can be sited "off-shore" in a national register of companies which does not allow you to find out who is the ultimate parent Corporation (i.e. you cannot find out who, theoretically, should be responsible).

A subsidiary Commercial Corporation can be created owning no assets. It can then decide for itself to accept the risk and responsibility of transporting crude oil and nuclear fuels (by air as well as by road and sea), running chemical plants, creating new drugs and herbicides, drilling and excavating sensitive areas.

At all times this subsidiary corporate person bears the sole responsibility for its actions. If anything goes wrong, the subsidiary simply folds and disappears. The

---

3 This is often referred to as "the corporate veil". A consideration of how subsidiaries developed and how the Courts have treated the relationship between parents and subsidiary corporations would justify a whole article to itself.

parent corporation, investors and directors know that, should anything go wrong, we are not entitled to look beyond the veil of the subsidiary Corporate person to see if the real persons who took those decisions should have been allowed to do so.[4]

Whilst Corporations (as legal persons) do not have the right to vote, they do have the right to lobby and fund political parties. They choose to pollute and exploit natural resources not only in their own land but in other lands, often without their new neighbours having any say over their presence. Corporations also have enormous influence in determining the manner in which resources are allocated and the nature of their products and markets. Whilst it is in the public's interest that resources be used sparingly and in a sustainable reusable manner, Corporations choose to create disposable products which require constant replacement/repurchase. The Corporations' interest in maximising sales and profits is in direct conflict with our own democratic right to choose how finite resources are allocated.

Modern Corporations are given not just the right to exploit resources but also the right to choose how they are exploited, marketed and packaged leaving the public with only the right to choose the method of cleaning up the mess left behind.

As neighbours of these Corporate Persons (in that we share the same environment and society) and as citizens, why do we have so little say how Corporations use their rights and powers? Why is it that these Corporate persons have no responsibility for their actions?

Not-for-profit corporations

The fiction of a corporation being a distinct legal person does exist for other collections of people. The concept of the corporation was initially created for charities such as churches, schools and universities, clubs, hospitals and so on and then latterly extended to municipal councils. These "not-for-profit" corporations were, by their nature, intended to advance the public good.

Before the seventeenth century incorporation was used only as a tool for not-for-profit entities. By making a hospital (for instance) into a corporate person its function was simplified and difficulties that could otherwise occur when control passed to later generations (death duties, transfer of assets etc.) could be avoided. It clearly served the public good for the long-term administration of such bodies to be simple.

Not-for-profit corporations had constitutions drafted and approved by the Crown or the Government, which set out their powers and the objects the corporation

---

4 The "Torrey Canyon" oil disaster of the Isles of Scilly in 1967 was an example of this. When the UK Government sought to recoup the clean up costs from the ship owner and cargo owner, it found that both never had any assets.

sought to attain. If a corporation acted outside its constitution (i.e. sought to attain an objective not within its objects or not within the spirit of its constitution), it was acting "ultra vires" and the Court had the power to declare the offending action void and unlawful. Before the development of Commercial Corporations, this doctrine of ultra vires was relatively simple but rarely used . But, making a profit (for what was always a charitable organisation) was clearly ultra vires.

Unincorporated businesses such as cooperatives or partnerships (including law, accountancy and architects firms) have no legal identity of their own. Each partner retains a share of responsibility for the actions and decisions taken. The name of their business remains, before the law, merely a name by which to identify the collective.

Brief History of Corporate Development

The development of Commercial Corporations occurred in three waves. First, when the financial demands of colonial expansion grew too great, Commercial Corporations started to appear (explained later!). After their initial appearance, Corporations were created by the Crown[5] through Royal Charter ("Chartered Corporations") in the 1600s and early 1700s to carry out the business of "merchant adventuring" or "colonial plunder" (choose according to your political viewpoint).

Commercial Corporations reduced greatly in number after the South Sea Bubble in 1720 until there was a second wave of development with the creation of Corporations by Act of Parliament to build canals, waterworks and later railways from the end of the 1700s onwards. General business activity was carried out through non-corporate forms.

The third wave of development occurred following the Joint Stock Companies Act of 1844. This allowed Corporations to be created by a simple act of registration. It is this "Registered Corporation" which is the modern form that we recognise.[6]

First Wave (1600 - 1720)

Before the seventeenth century this fiction of a corporation being a distinct legal person did exist but only for not-for-profit entities. The concept of the corporation

5 The "Crown" means the King or Queen or (in the modern context) the Officers/Servants of the King or Queen.
6 This discussion of the history of the development of the commercial corporation is brief and misses many key points. For a more in-depth analysis (but from a pro-corporation/anti-democratic perspective) - see Holdsworth History of English Law Vol 8; Formoy The Historical Foundations of Modern Company Law; DuBois The English Business Company After the Bubble Act 1720 -1800; Hunt The Development of the Business Corporation in England 1800-1867; Gower Principles of Modern Company Law.

was initially[7] created for charities such as churches, schools and universities, clubs, hospitals and so on and then latterly extended to municipal councils. These "not-for-profit" corporations were, by their nature, intended to advance the public good.

By making a hospital (for instance) into a corporate person its function was greatly simplified. The hospital could own buildings and land in its own name and buy resources and employ labour without exposing individual trustees to financial risk. It clearly served the public good for the long-term administration of such bodies to be simple. All these corporations had constitutions drafted and approved by the Crown or the Government, which set out their limited powers and the objects the corporation sought to attain. If a corporation acted outside its constitution (i.e. sought to attain an objective not within its objects or not within the spirit of its constitution), it was acting "ultra vires" and the Court had the power to declare the offending action void and unlawful. Before the development of Commercial Corporations, this doctrine of ultra vires was relatively simple but rarely used.[8]

Businesses at this time typically involved small numbers of people operating as partners, sharing the risks of the business. Each partner retained individual responsibility for all the actions of the partnership. Unincorporated businesses such as cooperatives or partnerships (including most law, accountancy and architects firms to this day) had no legal identity of their own. Each partner retained responsibility for the debts and decisions collectively taken. The name of their business remained, before the law, merely a name by which to identify the collective.

Towards the end of the 1500s Charters of Incorporation from the Crown were granted to trade associations. These trade associations did not carry out trade in their own names but were also not-for-profit corporations. The Crown would grant the trade association a monopoly over a narrow area of trade.[9] Business partners could become "members" of the trade association so entitling them to carry out business in that trade.9 However, each business would trade independently, with each business's partners sharing ownership of their own business's stock with the partners remaining individually responsible for their business's actions.

The East India Company received its Royal Charter in 1600. When incorporated it too was merely a trade association, its members having the right to a monopoly on trade in "the Indies". A business partnership could become a member of the East India Company and so be licensed to trade to and from the Indies. During the course of the century, all the individual member/ partners started to amalgamate their stock until they became one big partnership owning all the stock jointly. That

7 It appears that this idea of incorporation came to Britain following the Norman invasion in 1066.
8 Suttons Hospital Case [1612] 10 Co Rep 30b is a rare example. For an in depth analysis of the development of ultra vires law see Street A Treatise of the Doctrine of Ultra Vires.
9 Early examples included watchmakers' and printers' guilds.

is, the East India Company had only one partnership operating within it carrying out all the trade.

Later in the seventeenth century[10], the stock from being owned collectively by all the member-partners, became owned instead by the East India Company itself. The partners (who were all members of the corporation in its nature as a trading association) swapped their shared ownership of the stock of the business partnership for a share in the "Joint Stock" of the corporation itself. So the East India Company came to be the first corporation to operate for a profit. The first Commercial Corporation, (or Joint Stock Company) owned by shareholding members, carrying out trade in the name of the Corporation.

The first Joint Stock Company or Commercial Corporation was created by the actions of its members alone. Not by the Government or the Courts or the public deciding it was a good idea but simply by the members of the East India Company choosing to act in that manner. As a result, there was neither debate on the ethics of allowing a business association to use the corporate form nor consideration of how this development might affect the public in general. The East India Company was undoubtedly exercising powers not within its constitution (i.e. "ultra vires") by operating for a profit. However, no one appears to have challenged this.

Trading as a Commercial Corporation offered clear advantages over partnerships. The Corporation continued to exist even if the original partners died or transferred their shares. The Corporation could bring and defend legal actions in its own name rather than the names of the partners. If one shareholder became bankrupt, company assets could not be used to pay his debts as company assets belonged to the Corporation (its own separate legal person) and not the shareholder. Although not fully realised at the time, if the Corporation couldn't pay its debts, shareholders own assets could not really be used to pay the debts of the company. However, the Courts did customarily allow creditors to sue the shareholders and directors when a Corporation could not pay its debts (unimaginable today).

The corporate form drew what the Courts describes as a "veil" between the actions of the Corporation and the people directing it. This differed greatly from partners in a partnership or cooperative, who remained at all times individually and collectively responsible for the partnership's actions.

Over the course of the late 1600s until 1720 many other trade associations started to trade on joint stock so becoming Commercial Corporations. The Crown began to grant charters to new Corporations expressly for them to trade as Commercial Corporations. In boom economic times, new Corporations were formed by both

10 Despite all my searches, the exact date appears to be unclear within a range of 10-20 years..

Charter and Act of Parliament to develop new patents and domestic trade, by now asking for outside investors to provide the finance.

However, dubious Corporations were created and persons masqueraded as Corporations to fraudulently obtain investors money. The South Sea Bubble and other financial scandals in the early part of the eighteenth century caused enormous losses to investors. This led the Government to believe that action was needed to control corporate behaviour. These fictitious corporate persons were beyond the reach of the law. How could you jail or discipline a fictitious person. Also, the Corporations dealing with foreign trade such as the East India Company, Levant Company and Hudson Bay Company had become huge monopolies, effectively achieving the power of an occupier.

The Reforms of 1720

The Government responses were, first, to wind up or nationalise many of the Chartered Corporations, confiscating their territories. Then, to control fraudulent activity, the Government created the "Bubble Act" of 1720.[11]

This Act provided in section 18 that all commercial undertakings (both Corporations and partnerships) "tending to the common grievance, prejudice and inconvenience of His Majesty's subjects" would be illegal and void. The Act also banned speculative buying and selling of shares and outlawed stockbroking in such shares. After 1720 (until 1825) shares could only legally be sold to persons genuinely taking over a role in running the Corporation or partnership.

Second Wave (1720 - 1825)

Between 1720 and 1844 new businesses that might previously have sought incorporation were operated as partnerships. Investigations into the old Corporations found many instances of fraud and a large number collapsed due to debts. Crown Servants became reluctant to grant Charters for new Commercial Corporations fearing that their creations would fall foul of the Bubble Act. However, the Bubble Act was rarely used. Only one prosecution under the Act is reported to have occurred. The general public did not have the resources to use the Act and the State did not appear to have the desire.

Parliament at first was wary of creating new Corporations by Act of Parliament. However, there was a public need for canals and waterworks to be built and the State did not have the money to finance such schemes without the assistance of outside

---

11 Geo 1, cap 18.

financiers. This led to parliamentary approval for specific Corporations to be created by Act of Parliament ("Statutory Corporations"). These Corporations where similar to those founded to build the Channel Tunnel and develop Docklands in recent years. An Act of Parliament would authorise the creation of a Corporation for a specific and narrow purpose and allow it to borrow money and bring and defend legal actions in its own name (so protecting the financiers from personal responsibility should the Corporation fail).

The general view at the time was that Corporations should only be created for very specific purposes. Adam Smith, the economist so favoured by modern Conservatives, commented in 1776 that the only trades that justified incorporation were banking, insurance, canal building and waterworks. He believed it was contrary to the public interest for any other businesses or trades to be incorporated and that all should be run as partnerships.[12]

Third Wave (1825 - 1989)

Between 1825 and 1856 a series of Acts of Parliament abandoned the controlled formation of Corporations and created the modern Registered Corporation. Two Presidents of the Board of Trade, Huskisson and more importantly, Gladstone sponsored these moves. The aim was widescale liberalisation of the market – often called "laissez-faire" capitalism. Both these men were born in Liverpool, then the richest city in the world from profits of the recently abolished slave trade[13] and other colonial trades. Those who campaigned for greater freedoms for corporate persons were more ambivalent to the freedoms of real persons.

In 1825 the Bubble Act was repealed[14], allowing shares to be traded freely. The Joint Stock Companies Act of 1844[15] created the modern form of Corporation for general business and trade. Via a simple process of registration, a Corporation with its own legal identity could be created ("Registered Corporation") to carry out a stated commercial activity. The Corporation would be required to register its constitution including an "objects clause" stating its purpose. However, the founders of the Corporation were free to decide the Corporation's purposes and limitations. The debate in the House of Commons records Gladstone stating:

Joint Stock Companies at present could not be formed with any privilege such as that of suing and being sued, except, by coming to Her Majesty in Council, or by applying to Parliament Under this Bill, there would be a power for the first time,

12 Adam Smith, *Wealth of Nations*, vol V, Chap 1, Part III, Art. 1.
13 Abolished by the Great Emancipation Act of 1833.
14 6 Geo 4. Cap. 91.
15 An Act for the Registration, Incorporation and Regulation of joint Stock Companies 7 & * Vic Cap 110.

for persons to associate themselves in companies, for the purpose of commercial pursuits, without the fear of interference from any human being whatsoever.[16]

The intention of the bill was clearly to grant the corporate person civil and human rights. The risks associated with allowing this freedom to fictitious persons were downplayed. *Hansard* goes on to state:

> Mr Parker agreed that great harm had been done by the abuse of the principles of Joint-Stock Companies; but one great principle distinguishing this country from others was the non-interference of the Government with the regulations of trade.[17]

Initially, these new Registered Corporations did not have limited liability. If the Corporation could not pay its debts, creditors could recover their money from the shareholders. However, following 10 years of debate, in 1855 an Act was passed[18] limiting shareholders liability to the amount they had paid for their shares (i.e. once the shares are paid for, a shareholder had no further responsibility for any debts or actions of the Corporation).

The debates include two interesting instances of the State's view of who the public was. In 1850, a select committee reported on *Investments for the Savings of the Middle and Working Classes*.[19] This report argued that limited liability for company shareholders was in the interests of the poor.

The idea was that the poor could buy shares for their own purposes and limited liability would protect them. What was not considered was what would happen when Corporations with limited liability could not (for instance) pay wages? When a Corporation collapses we are given the choice between shareholders bearing the cost or the employees bearing the cost. A limited liability scheme clearly chose the employees to bear the cost. A similar choice had to be made when a bank cannot repay its savers' money. Again, limited liability favours the bank's shareholders over its customers.

Another argument used in favour of limited liability was that by adding the word "limited" or "ltd" after the name of the Corporation, anyone dealing with the Corporation would know that they were dealing with a corporate person and not a real person. They would then know the risks they were facing and had the "choice" whether or not to deal with the Corporation. Whilst this may be true for lenders and

16 *Hansard* - Jul 3 1844, p 277.
17 *Hansard* - Jul 3 1844, p 278.
18 An Act for Limiting the Liability of Members of certain Joint Stock Companies 18 & 19 Vict. Cap 132 p993.
19 1850 BPP Vol XIX 169.

other traders, employees and neighbours of a Corporation have little choice. Further, those who put forward these arguments failed to foresee the day when corporate persons would carry out all business activity.

No one ever considered the idea that Corporations could spawn subsidiary Corporations to carry out the dirty work.

Rights to Challenge Corporate Behaviour

Before the proliferation of railway companies created by Act of Parliament (Statutory Corporations) and the 1844 Act allowing Registered Companies, the ultra vires rule (which allows Court challenges to excesses of corporate power) was seldom used. Officially, whilst a Corporation had all the rights of a person, it could perform no acts nor enter into transactions other than that which sprang naturally out its objects.[20]

One of the problems with English law is that so much of it is based on the precedent of previous cases. Once a case has been decided, its decision (or judgment) is law. However, if a case has not been brought on any area for a long time, the weight of the precedent diminishes. Accordingly, the power of the Courts to use the doctrine of ultra vires against Corporations was unclear.

Between 1846 and 1875, a series of cases concerning the acts of Commercial Corporations came before the Courts. Through the course of these cases, the Judges made absolutely clear that the doctrine of ultra vires did apply to Commercial Corporations and that, ultimately, the Courts controlled corporate behaviour.[21]

The first cases concerned the railway Corporations created by Act of Parliament. In *East Anglian Railways Company v Eastern Counties Railways Co [1851]*[22] Lord Chief Justice Jervis stated:

> It is clear that the [Eastern Counties Railway Co] have a limited authority only, and are a corporation only, for the purpose of making and maintaining the railway sanctioned by the Act; and that their funds can only be applied for the purposes directed and provided for by the statute.

Adding support to this, in *Shrewsbury Railway Company v L&NW Railway Company [1853]*[23] Lord Justice Turner stated:

20 HA Street, *A Treatise on the Doctrine of Ultra Vires*, p 7.
21 It must be stressed that the general public did not bring these cases. Until very recently, the cost of using the Courts made the law inaccessible to most people.
22 [1851] 11 C.B. p775 at p881.
23 [1853] 4 De G M & G p132-3.

[T]hese bodies have no existence independent of the Acts which created them, and they are created by Parliament with special and limited powers, and for limited purposes The fact of their being endued with such powers only shows that Parliament did not think fit to entrust them with more extended powers, or to incorporate them for other purposes.

Finally, leaving no doubt over the Court's control of Statutory Corporations, in *Eastern Counties Railways Company v Hawkes [1859]*[24], Lord Chief Justice Pollock stated that:

[A] Parliamentary Corporation is a corporation merely for the purposes for which it is established ; and it has no existence for any other purpose. Whatever is done beyond that purpose is ultra vires and void.

It was presumed that the new Registered Corporations created by the 1844 Act were also to be controlled by the Courts through the doctrine of ultra vires. As stated above, a Registered Corporation has, within its constitution, an "objects clause" which sets out what the Corporation was formed to do. However, by the 1844 Act, the Government had given the founders of these Corporations the power to create their own objects clause. Could the Courts, with the doctrine of ultra vires, still limit corporate behaviour?

In the first case of ultra vires of a *Registered Corporation, Riche v Ashbury Railway Carriage Company [1875]*[25], Lord Selborne confirmed the application of "ultra vires" to Registered Corporations, stating:

[C]ontracts for objects and purposes foreign to, or inconsistent with, [the objects clause] are ultra vires of the corporation itself.

Whilst accepting that a Corporation was a person before the law, the Courts also recognised that the corporate person was created for a specific purpose and it was within the Court's power to restrict and control the Corporation's actions to within that purpose.

However, there followed a series of developments that rendered the doctrine useless. First, in the case of *Bournemouth Corporation v Watts [1884]*[26] it was decided that outsiders could not use the doctrine of ultra vires to challenge corporate actions.[27]

24 [1859] 4 H&N p8 at p16.
25 [1875] LR 7 HL p653 at p694.
26 [1884] 14 QBD p87.
27 This case concerned a municipal corporation and a ratepayer but the decision also applied to commercial corporations.

With respect to Commercial Corporations, that limited the right to use the doctrine to shareholders and directors and, in limited circumstances, creditors of the Corporation.

With the Courts' insistence on maintaining the ultra vires rules, Commercial Corporations could not bulldoze past the Courts' power to decide what was or was not within their power. However, Corporate lawyers realised that the 1844 Act gave them the power to circumvent the Courts. New Registered Corporations gave themselves wide objects clauses, giving them power to do more and more and adding final clauses stating that:

> The objects specified in each paragraph of this clause shall be in no way limited or restricted by reference to or inference from the terms of any other paragraph or the name of the company.

Initially the Courts were not happy to give meaning to such clauses. In *Stephens v Mysore Reefs (Kangundy) Company [1902]*[28] Justice Swinfen Eady stated:

> It is not right to accept a construction which would virtually enable the company to carry on any business or undertaking of any kind whatsoever.

Between 1902 and 1965 case after case was brought before the Courts where Corporations had attempted to use wide, all encompassing objects clauses. Uncertainty grew over how widely a Commercial Corporation could draft its powers as Courts sometimes decided actions were ultra vires and sometimes not. Business leaders heavily criticised the Courts for their apparent indecision.

Eventually, the Court abandoned any attempt at control of Commercial Corporations in the case of *Bell Houses Limited v City Wall Properties Limited [1966]*[29] The Court of Appeal approved an objects clause giving the Corporation power to:

> Carry on any other trade or business whatsoever which can, in the opinion of the board of directors, be advantageously carried on by the company in connection with or as ancillary to any of the above businesses or the general business of the company...

---

28 [1902] 1 Chan p745.
29 [1966] 2 QB p693.

The effect of the so-called "Bell Houses clause" and the Court of Appeal's decision was to transfer the right to decide the limits of a Corporation's powers from the Courts to the Board of Directors of each Corporation.

The final demise of the doctrine of ultra vires (so far as it related to the restriction on the rights of Commercial Corporations) took place in the Companies Act 1989.[30] The Act maintained the requirement for Corporations to include a statement of their objects in the constitution. But, under section 3A, allowed the Corporation to (a) state simply that it was a "general commercial company" and (b) that the Corporation has "power to do all such things as are incidental or conducive to the carrying on of any trade or business by it".

Finally, section 35(1) of the same Act altered the law so that "the validity of an act done by a company shall not be called into question on the ground of lack of capacity by reason of anything in the company's [objects clause]".

And so the corporate persons were liberated from the last of the formal legal restraints on their rights. In theory, they can still be brought to book for their breaches of duty to the public as neighbours, just as we are to each other. However, with subsidiary Corporations holding all the duty and responsibility for corporate behaviour, this control is somewhat illusionary.

Over the course of approximately 300 years, the State, which initially was very wary of allowing Corporations to have profitable motives, relinquished every one of the mechanisms it had in place to allow the public interest to overrule corporate interest. When disempowering the public, the only debate concerned Corporations' right to be free. This was largely presumed by those making the changes to be in the public's interest.

---

30 This Act applied only to Commercial Corporations. The law relating to charitable corporations has not changed that much since 1612.

The Human Rights Act and Corporations ...
or ...
"Why Human Rights aren't just for humans"

From 2 October 2000, there has been a Human Rights Act in this country. The Act was the incorporation into UK law of the European Convention on Human Rights.

What are Human Rights (very briefly)

The concept of what are Rights and who is given their protection against whom has changed over time.

Human Rights are popularly considered to have arisen in the Magna Carta, signed by King John in 1215. This is considered the first legal document which sought to restrain the power of monarchs over their subjects. Rights were awarded only to property-owning Englishmen (i.e. the Barons) and consisted mainly of restrictions on the King's interference with the Barons' land, produce, capital and servants. However, it did also protect the Baron's "civil" rights to life, liberty and freedom from detention without speedy trial.

By the 1790's, revolutions in the USA and France had taken this concept further, drafting constitutions professing to guarantee the protection of individual people (citizens) from abuse by the State of its powers. Initially these rights were restricted by property-ownership, race, gender, religion and, nationality. But, what was important was that these new expressions of Rights protected "political" freedoms. The constitutions sought to restrict the state from preventing (and required the promotion of) freedom of speech, association, movement, access to participation in public office etc.

In 1948, the United Nations extended Rights twofold. The Universal Declaration of Human Rights made the right to Rights inalienable (i.e. it was not possible to argue that any individual was not entitled to a particular Right by reason of their status).

More controversially, the Declaration introduced the concept of "social, economic and cultural" Rights. These included many workplace Rights to fair wages, safe and healthy conditions, rest and holiday and equality in promotion. Also included were Rights to a safe and healthy environment, equality of access to the benefits of scientific and technical progress, freedom to follow one's own cultural life and need-based access to world food supplies.

In the face of opposition from the North Western nations, it took 20 years for the UN to complete its task of clarifying the Universal Declaration on Human

Rights. This was done through splitting Rights into two groups. One covenant dealt with civil and political Rights, similar in nature to the US and French constitutions. A second was left to deal with the economic, social and cultural Rights. The final insult was for the North Western nations to succeed in classifying the latter as aspirational in nature and not intended to be existent Rights.

Where does the UK Human Rights Act fit in?

The UK Human Rights Act brings us into line with the US and French position 200 years ago, steering clear of all reference to social, economic and cultural Rights.

Where do Corporations fit in?

In law there are only two entities, the State and People. Everything is either a part of the state (e.g. ministries, hospital trusts, councils etc.) or a person or group of people (e.g. members clubs, partnerships, cooperatives etc.). The whole concept of Rights aimed to protect people from the abuse of state power. Accordingly, it could only be used by people against the state.

Corporations are treated as people under the law. This has two distinct and important effects. The Courts must allow a corporation, as a matter of law, to claim entitlement to "human" Rights when in dispute with the state.

Second, as a corporation is considered a person, a real person cannot object that a corporation's action breaches their human Rights as only the actions of a State (or part of it) can, by definition, be in breach of human Rights.

How could corporations use Human Rights?

It is farcical to attribute many of the human Rights to corporations. The civil rights of freedom from torture, slavery, imprisonment require a physical, living body to be in danger in the first place. However, the political rights of freedom of thought, expression, association and access to justice can and are used to defend corporate funding of political parties, lobbying and influence of governmental licensing and safety bodies and, use of the Court system for injuncting human opponents.

But, the most feared of all Rights by lawyers is the right to peaceful enjoyment of possessions (1st Protocol, Article 1) - in essence, a human property Right and considered a civil right. It is this right which is already used by corporations to prevent (or threaten) planning committees seeking to intervene in building and development plans. With cash-strapped local councils, the threat of litigation with a large corporation is often as decisive as a court victory.

Anticipate use of this Right when any patent or invention is up for discussion and the government is considering "interfering" in the corporations freedom to use its intellectual property; when toxic or hazardous industries are proposed on corporate owned land; when regulation of private utilities is suggested; when deforestation or chemical treatment of or experimentation on land is taking place.

The absence of any social, economic or cultural Rights for the public as a counterpoint to corporate use of human civil and political Rights threatens matters further. When corporations bring Human Rights actions against the state in the courts, without the appropriate Rights of its own, the public will have no right to intervene. The first we will hear of these cases is likely to be when the court decision is publicised.

The Corporate Liability Shuffle

Corporations are adept at avoiding responsibility when risky ventures collapse. Frustrating though this may be to those on the receiving end of corporate misdemeanours it is all perfectly legal and above board.

Simple parent - subsidiary

The Torrey Canyon oil tanker ran aground in the English Channel in March 1967, polluting coastlines of England and France. When the UK Government sued the ship owner and the cargo owner for the costs of an expensive clean-up operation, it discovered that both owners were penniless and had never possessed any assets at all other than the oil and the ship, both of which were lost. Worse still, they were resident in flag-of-convenience states, where no-one could discover which parent company owned the guilty subsidiaries.

This model of corporate evasion is simple and adaptable. When a ship leaves the dock, it is chartered to a subsidiary corporation with no assets. This corporation agrees to take all responsibility should anything go wrong. The same applies to the oil from the moment it 'crosses the rail' of the ship, with automatic transfer of ownership on arrival at its destination.

All ships are run this way. All dangerous cargoes are transported in this manner. In fact, all corporations run all risky activities through subsidiaries according to these rules.

Conglomerate liability shuffle

When a large company takes over a small one, you would expect the larger to buy all the assets of the smaller, so that the smaller would cease to exist. Wrong. If that were so, the larger company could be held responsible for the smaller's misdemeanours. Buildings badly constructed by the smaller company might collapse. Workers exposed to harmful substances might become ill or die. And the larger company would be responsible. Instead, the game runs something like this. When a large company buys a small one, the shares of the small company ('A') are bought by an even smaller company existing within the same group of companies('B'). This smaller company has typically been bought some time before but no longer trades.

However, B buys A's shares not with its own money but with money loaned to B from C (yes, another company like B). In return for loaning the money for the shares, C is given a mortgage or charge over everything that A owns. The result of this is that if anyone wishes to sue A, they will find themselves behind C in the queue for the money.

Matters do not end there. Any assets A had are bought by D with a loan from E, with E not actually giving A any money but with A agreeing to accept an IOU from F, to whom E owes money. D then passes the assets from A to company G, to whom D owed money from a previous deal.

Confused? Try multiplying this process throughout a corporate structure involving hundreds of dormant companies (dormant except for these intra-group deals).

Question: When A's employees start dying from asbestos exposures, who do they sue?

Answer: They attempt to follow the tracks of liability through the conglomerate shuffle — to a standard of proof that must be acceptable in court.

Shell parent company

This relatively new strategy is intended to counter the obvious response to the conglomerate liability shuffle. Suing the parent company was the classic way of snuffling the shuffle. A parent company must have planned its shuffle, and only it could know the culprit. But what if the parent company has no assets?

Traditionally, corporate structures were designed in the form of pyramids. At the top was the public company (Plc) with the money and the power. In recent years, the Plc part of the corporate group moved down the pyramid, passing ownership of all its shares to a private holding company, and giving the public less access to the top.

This reached its logical conclusion when the purchase of the Plc's shares by the private company changed from being a two-party to a three-party affair.

Imagine a public company called X Plc. It is to sell its shares to Y Ltd. However, Y Ltd buys the X Plc shares with £10 million loaned to it by Z Ltd. In return, Z Ltd is given a mortgage or charge over all X Plc's assets. And, as we know, if anyone now sues X Plc, they will be looking at Z Ltd's backside all the way. Even if they try to sue Y Ltd, they will find that Y Ltd owes Z Ltd £10 million, and it wants paying first.

Doesn't X Plc still have the £10 million? That would be too easy. You see, Z Ltd kept the money and simply agreed to pay it sometime in the future. And you can't sue Z Ltd as they are completely outside the corporate group, are registered in the Turks and Caicos Islands, and know nothing about your collapsed building.

This model of corporate structure - except for the Turks & Caicos bit - is currently that of T&N Ltd, formerly T&N Plc before the reshuffle. T&N Ltd were the UK's biggest importer, manufacturer and installer of asbestos products into the 1990s, despite knowing about the dangers of asbestos since the 1920s. With an average lag between exposure and injury of 38 years and a maximum of 60, T&N's workers, neighbours and consumers will continue to die in large numbers for years. Despite the billions in profit made by T&N, many may find their claims being made against an assetless company.

Approaches to corporations

There are five ways to approach the question of corporations. Only three are ever discussed with any frequency. The remaining two, whilst being the most radical, tend to be ignored or unrealized

Pro-Corporation - The approach of those running corporations and their supporters is that corporations should be given total freedom - those running corporations should be entitled to take whatever actions and whatever risks necessary to make a profit.

Giving the corporation all the rights of a real person allows any business activity to be undertaken. Limiting the liability of the corporate person allows the taking of entrepreneurial risks that no real person could afford to take. This method produces the maximum profit. Any interference with the corporate form would hinder profit making and therefore harm society.

Liberal - Liberals recognise that the limit on the liability of those running corporations (directors and shareholders) allows them to take risks not just with capital but also with public welfare. It recognises that the complexity of corporate structures and the limits on their liability tends to put them beyond the law. This means that much of the cost of pollution, congestion and destruction caused by corporations are not borne by the corporations at all but by those individuals whose economic, social and cultural environment the corporation has entered. As corporations are not real people living amongst communities, they do not restrain their behaviour to avoid offending their neighbours.

Further, the corporate aim of maximisation of profit does not necessarily provide the benefits the public requires, as disposable products are created and scarce resources are plundered. The profit incentive of the corporation is often in direct conflict with the wider public welfare.

Liberals seek amendments to company law: e.g. imposing duties on directors of corporations to take into account environmental, social and cultural concerns when making their decisions. They also concentrate on consumer boycotts, hoping that the actions of consumers will replicate the role that neighbours play in ordinary society.

Socialist - Socialists recognise that the liberal approach, whilst restraining corporate behaviour to some extent through consumer boycotts, cannot deal with the wider effect corporations have on non-consumer groups such as environmental neighbours, local producers and anyone who did not want to buy the product in the first place. They recognise that the power of the boycott lies only in the hands of those with sufficient resources to be able to consume. Accordingly, the victims of corporate abuse rely on the support and patronage of those with purchasing power.

Socialists recognise that additional directors' duties will not help as the corporation retains the right to freedom of action and outsiders will not be permitted to interfere with its activities. Socialists see the alternative as state ownership of production to ensure that business is run for the benefit of society.

Democracy - The problem with state ownership of the means of production is that it replaces directors with bureaucrats who similarly have little interest in public welfare and little accountability. Those bureaucrats, whilst having all the powers of directors, have even less restraint on their activities. Further, it becomes impossible for anyone who wants to produce anything to do so freely and places the livelihoods of those who were independent and free from interference in the hands of the state. It becomes difficult to decide what should be put in public ownership and what should not.

This fourth approach recognises that corporations are the creations of the public, who recognise the need for certain business activities to be protected from crippling debts. Historically, this was how the canals and railways were developed - as no individual could take on the capital risk involved. Those corporations were considered as creations of the state to advance the public good, and they could accordingly be prevented from taking actions that would harm the public. Today this approach would make corporations subject to human rights law rather than entitled to its protection as virtual 'people'.

Real people could complain that corporations were infringing basic civil, political, economic, social and cultural rights and demand that such infringement cease. This view of corporations recognises that profit-making business can be for the public good but only if it is not allowed to harm the public welfare. Rather than allowing the rights of the corporate people to compete with and trump the rights of real people, instead corporations would have no human rights but could simply operate where and how the public allowed. This approach to corporations forms the basis of the campaign by the Program on Corporations, Law and Democracy in the USA.

Anarchy - This view recognises that a considerable problem with corporate activity is the absence of responsibility of those running the corporation. The corporate form allows (and in many situations obliges) the directors of the corporation to put profits before public welfare. And it may always be the case that where there is an opportunity for profit but also a risk to public welfare, the shield of the corporation allows its directors to take that risk.

The only way to re-establish the link between action and responsibility is to abolish the corporate form. Business and "free trade" can continue but only where those taking decisions and acting upon them are held individually responsible. Such a change would make it impossible for the large transnational companies to continue as the directors and shareholders would be unable to remain responsible for such wide ranging and costly risks and big business would disappear. However, small "business" — people making things and providing services — could still operate for profits. This approach to Corporation is the one proposed by Adam Smith in 1776 in *Wealth of Nations*.[31]

31 Adam Smith,*Wealth of Nations*, vol V, Chap 1, Part III, Art. 1.

THEY CAME FROM THE PLANET WALL STREET IN A HOSTILE BID TO TAKE OVER THE WORLD

INVASION OF THE CORPORATRONS

ARE Y-YOU THEIR L-LEADER?

NO, I'M HIS ATTORNEY. **TAKE ME TO YOUR ASSETS!**

ATM

THE CORPORATRONS HAD USED UP ALL THEIR RESOURCES...

...ON INDUSTRIAL GARBAGE DUMPS OF CARS, TELEVISIONS AND PLASTIC JUNK.

WHERE'S MY HAIR DRYER?

THEY NEEDED RAW MATERIALS (AND NEW CONSUMERS) TO MAKE MORE CRAP.

WE'RE OUT OF WATER, MINERALS, OIL, AIR AND ...SODA!

UH-OH... NO DIET PEPSI!?

SO THEY DECIDED TO **INVADE** THE **EARTH**!

IT HAS ENORMOUS MARKETING POTENTIAL

EARTH

THE CORPORATRONS DESCENDED ON THE EARTH IN LEXUS AND BMW FLYING SAUCERS.

USING TELEVISIONS WITH ENDLESS ADVERTISING AND BAD PROGRAMMING, THEY HYPNOTIZED EVERYONE...

... AND, THUS, ENSLAVED THE EARTH'S POPULATION IN DEMEANING JOBS.

HAVING GOTTEN THE EARTHLINGS HOOKED ON USELESS CONSUMER GOODS,

ANIMALS, MINERALS, PLANTS, SOIL, AIR AND WATER WERE ALL NEEDED BACK HOME FOR MANUFACTURING.

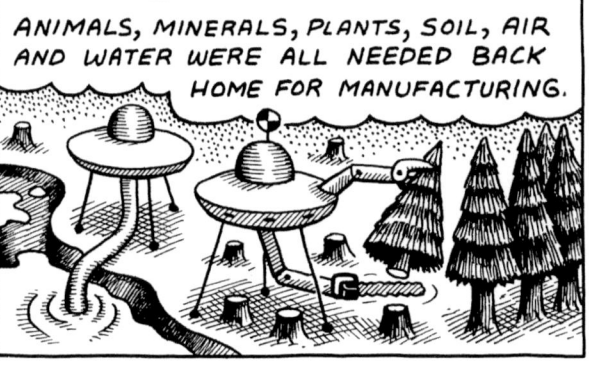

THE CORPORATRONS BEGAN EXTRACTING EARTH'S NATURAL RESOURCES.

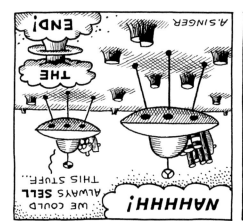

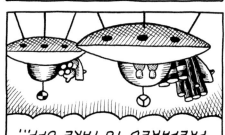
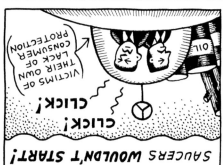